cobblers & crumbles

cobblers & crumbles

Maxine Clark

photography by Peter Cassidy

RYLAND
PETERS
& SMALL

LONDON NEW YORK

Senior Designer Steve Painter
Commissioning Editor Julia Charles
Production Gordana Simakovic
Art Director Anne-Marie Bulat
Publishing Director Alison Starling

Food Stylists Maxine Clark & Linda Tubby
Prop Stylist Róisín Nield
Index Hilary Bird

Dedication
To E.P.S. and I.R.E.C.

Author's Acknowledgments
Special thanks to the photographic team—
Peter, Róisín, Steve, and Linda—for struggling
with winter light, finding sympathetic props,
finding out-of-season ingredients from near
and far, and preparing yummy-looking
desserts. Thanks, as always, to Sharon and
Julia at RPS for their good-natured patience,
humor, and meticulous editing skills

First published in the United States
in 2006 by Ryland Peters & Small, Inc.
519 Broadway, 5th Floor
New York, NY 10012
www.rylandpeters.com

10 9 8 7 6 5 4 3 2 1

Text © Maxine Clark 2006
Design and photographs
© Ryland Peters & Small 2006

Printed in China

Library of Congress Cataloging-in-
Publication Data

Clark, Maxine.
  Cobblers & crumbles / Maxine Clark ;
photography by Peter Cassidy. -- 1st ed.
    p. cm.
  Includes index.
  ISBN-13: 978-1-84597-214-1
  ISBN-10: 1-84597-214-7
  1. Desserts. 2. Cookery (Fruit) I. Title. II.
Title: Cobblers and crumbles.
  TX773.C5635 2006
  641.8'6--dc22

2006008834.

Notes
• All spoon measurements are level, unless
otherwise specified.
• Eggs are US extra-large unless otherwise
specified.
• Ovens should be preheated to the
specified temperatures. All ovens work
slightly differently. We recommend using
an oven thermometer and suggest you
consult the maker's handbook for any
special instructions—particularly if you are
using a fan-assisted oven as you may need
to adjust cooking temperatures.
• The size of baking pan given in each
recipe is most often expressed as small,
medium, or large.The pans used for recipe
testing were as follows:
Individual— 3-inch diameter (round)
Small—8 x 6 inch (oval)
Medium—9 x 7 inch (oval)
Large—11 x 8½ inch (oval)
Please be aware that cooking times may
vary depending on the size, shape, depth,
and material of the pan you use.

contents

introduction

Everyone loves a good fruit Cobbler. The name supposedly originates from the "cobbled" effect on the surface of the fruit made by the circles of sweet dough. The permutations are endless—from soft dropped doughs to firmer shortcake-like toppings. The aptley named Slump has either a soft topping that is very rustic in appearance, and is spooned over the fruit, or the topping mixture is used for a base with the fruits scattered and embedded in it. The Pandowdy is something quite different again—a soft pie crust draped over the entire dish then baked. The crust is broken up just before serving so that the pieces absorb the fruit juices making it the perfect recipe if you aren't skilled at pastry-making!

I personally couldn't imagine life without a crumble. It's one of Britain's most enduringly popular desserts. If I am not sure what dessert to make, I rustle up a simple crumble with whatever fruit is in season and watch faces light up. A crumble is a satisfying mix of tart fruit and crumbly-crunchy topping made with the simplest of ingredients; flour, sugar, and butter. This mix can be endlessly adapted by varying the type of sugar from granulated to soft brown, or the type of flour from all-purpose to polenta. Crushed cookies add interest too, as do spices, and chopped nuts. Once you've mastered the basics, then the variations are yours to command. Crumbles do exactly what they say, they crumble and melt in the mouth. If more butter is used, the topping will melt and form a crust. Add more sugar and you will have a Crisp with a slightly crunchier topping, or a Betty, made with layers of crunchy sugary mixture and fruit.

Whichever type you choose, there is something for everyone here and all benefit from a good helping of cream, ice cream, or crème Anglaise to complete the idyll!

crumbles

Plums have such a rich flavor when they are cooked that they need little or no other flavorings with them, except perhaps a pinch of cinnamon. This is a favorite with kids—especially when made with greeny-red Victoria plums. Try it with greengages, Santa Rosas, or Queen Anne plums—they will all be delicious. For a grown-up crumble, toss the uncooked plums in a little damson or sloe gin.

simple plum crumble

8–10 ripe plums

4–5 tablespoons sugar

for the crumble topping:

½ stick plus 1 tablespoon unsalted butter, chilled

1⅓ cups all-purpose flour

a pinch of salt

¼ cup superfine sugar

a baking sheet

a medium, shallow, ovenproof dish

Serves 4-6

Preheat the oven to 350°F and set a baking sheet on the middle shelf to heat.

Cut the plums in half and remove the pits. Cut the halves into quarters if they are very large. Toss them with the sugar and tip them into an ovenproof baking dish.

To make the topping, rub the butter into the flour with the salt until it resembles rough bread crumbs. Alternatively do this in a food processor. Stir in the sugar. (At this point the mixture can be placed into a plastic bag and chilled until ready to cook.)

Lightly scatter the topping mixture over the plums. Place the baking dish on the baking sheet in the preheated oven and bake for 40–45 minutes until golden brown.

Remove from the oven and serve warm with light cream.

This luscious crumble is sophisticated enough for the best dinner party. Chocolate and pears were made for each other—here the chocolate melts and mixes with the pear juice to make a delicious sauce. Pumpernickel makes an interestingly crunchy topping, and gives the dessert a dramatic look.

pear and chocolate crumble

2–3 large not-too-ripe pears

¼ cup superfine sugar

2–3 tablespoons sweetened cocoa powder or grated bittersweet chocolate

finely grated zest of ½ a lemon

for the choco-pumpernickel topping:

4 oz. sliced pumpernickel

4 oz. stale brown bread

4 tablespoons sweetened cocoa powder or grated bittersweet chocolate

½ stick unsalted butter, chilled

⅓ cup light brown sugar

a baking sheet

a medium, shallow, ovenproof dish

Serves 4

Preheat the oven to 350°F and set a baking sheet on the middle shelf to heat.

Peel, core, and slice (or chop) the pears and put them in an ovenproof baking dish so that they fill it by two thirds. Sprinkle the sugar, sweetened cocoa (or grated chocolate if using) and lemon zest over the top and mix well to coat the pears. Cover and set aside.

To make the topping, tear up the pumpernickel and bread slices and put in the bowl of a food processor. Pulse for a minute or so until very roughly crumbed. Add the sweetened cocoa (or grated chocolate if using), butter, and sugar, and pulse again for a minute or so until finer crumbs form. Do not over-blend or it will form a solid lump. Place in a plastic bag and chill in the fridge until needed.

When ready to cook the crumble, uncover the pears and sprinkle lightly and evenly with the topping mixture. Place the baking dish on the baking sheet in the preheated oven and bake for 25–30 minutes, until the pears are very tender and the top nice and crisp.

Remove from the oven and serve warm with light cream or a scoop of chocolate ice cream.

The halved pears act as an edible dish in this recipe. It is really important to caramelize the cut side of the pears to a dark mahogany to bring out their full flavor. Don't add too much egg to the almond mixture—it must be quite lumpy so that it doesn't flow out of the pears as it cooks. Easy to prepare in advance, these make a spectacular winter dinner party dessert.

caramelized pear and bourbon crumbles with frangipane topping

2 large pears

¼ cup sugar

4 tablespoons bourbon

1 stick less 1 tablespoon unsalted butter

for the frangipane topping:

1 cup ground almonds

⅓ cup chopped almonds

⅔ cup superfine sugar

extra splash of bourbon

1 egg, beaten

½ cup sliced almonds

a medium, shallow, ovenproof dish

Serves 4

Preheat the oven to 375°F.

Cut the pears in half, and scoop out the cores. Melt the sugar in a heavy skillet and cook until a good dark caramel. Splash in the bourbon, then add the pears, cut-side down, with the butter. Cook over medium heat for 10 minutes or until the cut side of the pears turns a rich dark brown. Remove from the heat and arrange the pears, cut-side up, in an ovenproof baking dish. Pour the cooking juices around the pears.

To make the frangipane topping, mix the ground almonds, chopped almonds, and superfine sugar with a splash of bourbon and enough beaten egg until it begins to clump together. Mound this mixture on top of the baked pears and scatter with the sliced almonds. Bake in the preheated oven for 20–25 minutes, until golden.

Remove from the oven, spoon over the caramelized juices and serve warm with whipped cream or vanilla ice cream.

If you have frozen blackberries in the freezer there is no need to defrost them—they will cook from frozen once in the crumble. It is important to bake the crumble in a moderate oven for a long time as this is what gives the topping its wonderful crunch.

4–5 medium cooking apples

½ lb. blackberries
(fresh or frozen)

¼ cup superfine sugar

¼ teaspoon apple pie spice

finely grated zest and juice of
½ a lemon

for the crumble topping:

1¾ sticks unsalted butter, chilled

1½ cups all-purpose flour

a pinch of salt

⅓ cup light brown or white sugar

a baking sheet

a large, shallow, ovenproof dish

Serves 6

classic blackberry and apple crumble

Preheat the oven to 350°F and set a baking sheet on the middle shelf to heat.

Peel, core, and slice the apples and put them in a mixing bowl. Add the blackberries, sugar, apple pie spice, lemon zest and juice, and toss well to mix. Turn into an ovenproof baking dish.

To make the crumble, rub the butter into the flour with the salt until it resembles rough bread crumbs. Alternatively do this in a food processor. Stir in the sugar. (At this stage the mixture can be placed in a plastic bag and chilled in the fridge until ready to cook.) Lightly scatter the topping mixture over the apples and blackberries. Place on the baking sheet in the preheated oven and bake for 50–60 minutes.

Remove from the oven and serve warm with light cream or Crème Anglaise (see page 63.)

For me, summer has truly arrived when I taste gooseberries. They are my favorite fruit and seem to have a natural affinity with ginger. Ginger wine is a delicious tipple and it really brings out the flavor of the gooseberries. I like to cook the fruit a little first to draw out the excess liquid (as it would make the crumble too wet) but I keep it to warm and serve with the cooked dish.

gooseberry and ginger wine crumble

2 lbs. green gooseberries, trimmed

3 tablespoons ginger wine

½ cup superfine sugar

for the ginger topping:

1½ cups all-purpose flour

1 teaspoon powdered ginger

a pinch of salt

1 stick unsalted butter, chilled and cut up

½ cup superfine sugar

a baking sheet

a medium, shallow, ovenproof dish

Serves 4

Preheat the oven to 375°F and set a baking sheet on the middle shelf to heat.

Place the gooseberries in a non-reactive saucepan, add the ginger wine and sugar, and cook gently until the fruit starts to burst. Remove from the heat and tip the gooseberries into a strainer set over a clean pan to catch the juices. Next tip the gooseberries into an ovenproof baking dish, covering the bottom with a single layer. Reserve the juices for later.

Next make the topping. Put the flour, ginger, salt, and butter into a food processor and blend until it looks like coarse bread crumbs. (Alternatively you can rub it in by hand.) Tip into a mixing bowl and stir in the sugar.

Lightly sprinkle the topping mixture evenly over the prepared gooseberry mixture, mounding it up a little towards the center. Place the baking dish on top of the baking sheet in the preheated oven and bake for about 25 minutes, until crisp and golden on top.

Remove from the oven and allow to cool for 5 minutes before serving with the warmed reserved juices and whipped cream.

Some cooks like to remove the skins from the peaches before pitting them—I like to keep them on as they add color and texture to the finished dish. This can be made in individual shallow bowls or in one big dish, as you prefer. As it is quite buttery, it's best to serve it with any type of cream except ice cream.

peach and amaretti crumble

4–6 large, firm but ripe peaches or nectarines

2 tablespoons Amaretto di Saronno liqueur or similar (optional)

for the amaretti topping:

9 oz. amaretti cookies

2 tablespoons syrup from a jar of candied or preserved ginger

1 egg yolk

2 tablespoons finely chopped candied or preserved ginger

¾ stick unsalted butter, chilled and cut up

a baking sheet

a medium, shallow, ovenproof dish

Serves 4

Preheat the oven to 375°F. Set a baking sheet on the middle shelf to heat.

Cut the peaches in half, remove the pits, then cut the peach halves into quarters. Toss with the Amaretto liqueur, if using. Arrange the peaches in the dish in a single layer, cut-side up.

Roughly crush the amaretti cookies in a plastic bag using a rolling pin. Mix the ginger syrup and egg yolk together and stir or lightly rub into the crushed cookies along with the chopped ginger until the mixture looks quite lumpy and rough. Scatter this over the peaches, and don't worry if it doesn't completely cover them. Dot with butter and bake for 20–25 minutes, until tender and the top is brown and crisp.

Remove from the oven and serve warm with crème fraîche, sour cream, or heavy cream.

This is a very useful recipe for when nectarines are slightly hard, as cooking them softens the flesh and brings out the flavor. Ginger goes particularly well with this fruit so I've used ginger cookies here but if they are not available, simply substitute them with any favorite crunchy cookie and add a good pinch or two of ground ginger to the topping mixture.

nectarine and ginger crumble

6 medium-sized nectarines (or a mixture of peaches and plums)

2 tablespoons finely chopped candied or preserved ginger

5 tablespoons apple juice

¼ cup superfine sugar

for the ginger topping:

1 stick unsalted butter, melted

7 oz. gingersnap cookies, crushed

½ cup light brown sugar

a baking sheet

a medium, shallow, ovenproof dish

Serves 4

Preheat the oven to 375°F and set a baking sheet on the middle shelf to heat.

Cut the nectarines in half and remove the pits, then slice or chop them. Tip them into an ovenproof baking dish and mix with the chopped ginger, apple juice, and sugar.

Now make the ginger topping. Melt the butter in a saucepan and stir in the crushed cookies and sugar until the mixture resembles rough bread crumbs. (At this stage you can place it in a plastic bag and chill in the fridge until needed.)

Lightly sprinkle the topping mixture evenly over the surface of the nectarines, mounding it up a little towards the center.

Place the baking dish on top of the baking sheet in the preheated oven and bake for about 25 minutes, until crisp and golden on top.

Remove from the oven and let cool for 5 minutes before serving with vanilla ice cream or heavy cream.

There is a dessert in south-west France called *Pastis Gascon* which is essentially a buttery, handmade phyllo pastry apple or prune tart with a feather-light topping of sugar-dusted phyllo pastry, suffused with local fiery Armagnac. My version, a type of crumble, uses less pastry dough.

apple, prune, and armagnac phyllo crumble

4 sheets of ready-made phyllo dough

1 stick unsalted butter, melted

4 sweet apples

16 ready-to-eat pitted prunes

2–3 tablespoons Armagnac or cognac

3 tablespoons superfine sugar

finely grated zest of 1 lemon

confectioners' sugar, for dusting

a medium, shallow, ovenproof dish

Serves 4

Preheat the oven to 375°F.

Lay the phyllo dough out on a clean counter and brush with the melted butter. Leave to set and dry out for 15–20 minutes.

Meanwhile, peel, core, and slice the apples and quarter the prunes. Toss them together in a bowl with the Armagnac, sugar, and the lemon zest. Pile the fruit into an ovenproof baking dish, cover with tin foil, and bake in the preheated oven for about 20 minutes.

Scrunch the pastry dough up so that it rips and tears and breaks into small rags. Remove the apple and prune mixture from the oven and lightly scatter the phyllo pieces on top, making sure it looks quite ragged and spiky. Dust lightly with confectioners' sugar and bake for another 20 minutes, until golden brown.

Remove from the oven and serve warm with Crème Anglaise (see page 63).

The holiday season has definitely arrived when the smell of this crumble starts to drift around the house. A mixture of either traditional or exotic dried fruit provides a rich base for the light crumble topping. The spicy mulled wine seeps into the fruit as it cooks and plumps it up nicely. I like to serve this as a superior substitute for British mincemeat pies.

mulled winter fruit crumble

12 oz. mixed dried fruit (apples, apricots, figs, raisins, cranberries, mango, pineapple, pawpaw)

2 cups red wine

1 small cheesecloth bag of mulled wine spices (cinnamon, cloves, allspice)

strip of orange zest

¼ cup superfine sugar

for the spiced topping:

1½ cups whole-wheat flour

¼ teaspoon apple pie spice

a pinch of salt

1 stick unsalted butter, chilled and cut up

½ cup light brown sugar

a baking sheet

a medium, shallow, ovenproof dish

Serves 4

Preheat the oven to 375°F and set a baking sheet on the middle shelf to heat.

Chop the dried fruit into bite-sized pieces and place in a non-reactive saucepan. Add the wine, mulling spices, orange zest, and sugar. Heat gently, then simmer for 10 minutes. Set aside to cool.

Spoon the semi-cooked dried fruit into an ovenproof baking dish and remove the mulling spices and orange zest.

Now make the topping. Put the flour, apple pie spice, salt and butter into a food processor and blend until it looks like coarse bread crumbs. (Alternatively you can rub it in by hand). Tip the mixture into a bowl and stir in the sugar. (At this stage you can place it in a plastic bag and chill in the fridge until needed.)

Lightly sprinkle the topping mixture evenly over the surface of the dried fruit, mounding it up a little towards the center. Place on top of the baking sheet in the preheated oven and bake for about 25 minutes, until crisp and golden on top.

Remove from the oven and let cool for 5 minutes before serving with heavy cream.

Rhubarb is one of my favorite fruits (although it's really a vegetable!) It holds vivid childhood memories of dipping young raw rhubarb sticks into sugar and munching away, sitting amongst the huge leaves in my family's rhubarb patch. Orange seems to draw out and temper the sharp flavor with delicious results.

rhubarb and orange crumble

1½ lbs. fresh forced rhubarb (for its zing and color)

2 large oranges

a pinch of ground ginger

¾ cup superfine or light brown sugar

for the almond topping:

1 cup all-purpose flour

pinch of salt

⅔ cup ground almonds

1 stick unsalted butter, chilled

1 cup blanched almonds, chopped

¼ cup light brown sugar

a baking sheet

a medium, shallow, ovenproof dish or 4 individual dishes

Serves 4

Preheat the oven to 400°F and set a baking sheet on the middle shelf to heat.

Trim the rhubarb, cut it into large chunks, and place in a large saucepan. Finely grate the zest from the oranges and add to the rhubarb. Stir in the ground ginger and sugar and cook over a gentle heat for a few minutes, stirring occasionally until the rhubarb begins to release its juices but is still holding its shape. Pour the rhubarb into a strainer set over a bowl to catch the juices and reserve these for later. Remove the pith from the oranges with a sharp knife, then cut out the segments between the membrane. Add to the drained rhubarb and set aside to cool completely.

Now make the topping. Put the flour, salt, ground almonds, and butter into a food processor and blend until it looks like coarse bread crumbs. (Alternatively you can rub it in by hand.) Tip the mixture into a bowl and stir in the chopped nuts and sugar. (At this stage you can place it in a plastic bag and chill in the fridge until needed.)

Spoon the rhubarb and oranges into a large ovenproof dish or 4 individual ones. Lightly sprinkle the almond mixture evenly over the surface, mounding it up a little towards the center. Place on top of the baking sheet in the preheated oven and bake for about 35 minutes, until crisp and golden on top.

Remove from the oven and let cool for 5 minutes before serving with heavy cream and the warmed reserved juices.

These individual crumbles are a little complicated to make, but well worth the effort. Be very careful when transferring them from the pan to the plate—a trusty spatula will help. They make a spectacular dinner party dessert and a sophisticated alternative to banoffi pie!

toffee banana crumbles

8 bananas

¼ cup soft brown sugar

freshly squeezed juice of 1 lemon

for the coconut topping:

⅓ cup all-purpose flour

⅔ cup shredded unsweetened coconut

½ stick unsalted butter, chilled and cut up

2 tablespoons superfine sugar

a medium, cast iron, skillet

4 individual heatproof chef's rings (3-inch diameter)

Serves 4

Preheat the oven to 375°F.

Trim and cut the bananas into 1¼-inch lengths. Reserve 4 lengths for the centers of the crumbles, then slice each of the remaining ones in half lengthwise. Sprinkle the sugar into a heavy cast iron skillet, then place 4 chef's rings into the sugar. Pack each ring with an upright banana length. Next, tightly surround this with the split bananas (to resemble the petals of a flower) and pour the lemon juice over the bananas and sugar.

Now make the topping. Put the flour, coconut, and butter into a food processor and blend until it looks like coarse bread crumbs. Alternatively you can rub it in by hand. Tip into a bowl and stir in the sugar. (At this stage you can place the mixture into a plastic bag and chill in the fridge until needed.)

Fill each ring to the top with the coconut mixture. Place the skillet in the preheated oven and bake for 25 minutes, until golden. Remove from the oven, slip a spatula under each ring and lift them out of the skillet onto four warmed plates. Carefully remove the rings and serve with the remaining skillet juices spooned around the crumbles.

Serve warm with light cream, crème fraîche, or sour cream.

This is a back-to-front crumble. The crumble and mango are baked separately, then served together for maximum crunch. You can prepare this topping in bulk and store it in an airtight jar so that you can make a really exotic dessert in a snap. Serve coconut ice cream with this, if you can find it.

mango and coconut macaroon crumble

2 fresh ripe mangoes

finely grated zest and juice of 1 lime

for the coconut macaroon topping:

2 tablespoons whole wheat flour

3 tablespoons unsalted butter

½ cup shredded, unsweetened coconut

3 oz. macaroon or coconut macaroon cookies

3 tablespoons light brown sugar

2 non-stick baking sheets

4 small, shallow, ovenproof dishes

Serves 4

Preheat the oven to 400°F.

Peel the mangoes with a potato peeler. Slice the sides from the mangoes as near to the pit as possible, then slice or chop the flesh, including any still clinging to the pits. Toss this with the lime zest and juice and spoon into 4 ovenproof, individual serving bowls (these must be shallow, as the mango needs to go into something that heats up quite quickly). Set them on a nonstick baking sheet and put into the preheated oven to cook while you make the topping.

To make the topping, rub the flour, butter, and coconut together until it looks like bread crumbs. Lightly crush the macaroon cookies in a plastic bag, then stir into the coconut mixture with the sugar. Spread out onto a nonstick baking sheet and toast in the oven for 10–15 minutes, until crisp. Remove both sheets from the oven and sprinkle the toasted coconut macaroon topping over the hot mango.

Serve immediately with coconut or vanilla ice cream.

This crumble is based on a famous Scottish dessert, combining raspberries with toasted oatmeal, whisky, heather honey, and cream. If you are using frozen raspberries, there is no need to defrost them first. The oatmeal topping packs a satisfyingly toasty crunch.

cranachan crumble

1 12-oz punnet fresh or frozen raspberries

6 tablespoons liquid honey (heather honey if available)

½ cup heavy cream

2 tablespoons whisky

for the oatmeal topping:

¾ stick unsalted butter

¾ cup fine oatmeal

1 cup rolled oats (not instant)

a baking sheet

a medium, shallow, ovenproof dish

Serves 4-6

Preheat the oven to 375°F. Place a baking sheet on the middle shelf to heat.

Put the raspberries into the baking dish. Drizzle with 3 tablespoons of the honey and pour in the cream and whisky.

Now make the topping. Melt the butter and the remaining honey in a saucepan and stir in both types of oats. Stir until they start to clump together like clusters of granola.

Sprinkle this oat mixture evenly over the surface of the raspberries, mounding it up a little towards the center.

Place the baking dish on the baking sheet in the preheated oven and bake the crumble for about 20–25 minutes, until crisp and golden on top.

Let cool for 5 minutes before serving with whipped cream.

cobblers

If fresh cranberries cannot be found, buy dried ones and soak them for at least one hour in gently warmed cranberry juice before using.

cranberry and apple cobbler

1 lb. fresh or frozen cranberries or 7 oz. dried cranberries

1 lb. cooking apples

finely grated zest and juice of 1 small orange

pinch of ground cloves

for the cobbler topping:

½ stick unsalted butter, chilled

1¾ cups self-rising flour

a pinch of salt

¼ cup superfine sugar

about ⅔ cup milk, plus extra for glazing

a medium, shallow, ovenproof dish

Serves 4

Preheat the oven to 425°F.

Pick over the cranberries and wash them. Peel and core the apples, then slice them thickly. Put all but a cup of the cranberries and all the apples into a saucepan with the orange zest and juice and the cloves. Poach gently for 15 to 20 minutes, until the fruit is juicy and tender. Set aside to cool.

Roughly chop the remaining cranberries. Rub the butter into the flour and salt until it resembles fine bread crumbs. Stir in the sugar and chopped cranberries. Add the milk to the flour, mixing with a blunt knife to form a fairly soft, sticky dough. On a lightly floured counter, roll out until ¾ inch thick or slightly thicker. Cut out circles using a fluted 1½–2-inch cookie cutter.

Spoon the fruit into an ovenproof baking dish and arrange the pastry circles around the edge of the dish, overlapping them slightly and leaving a gap in the center. Brush the top of the pastry circles with milk. Bake in the preheated oven for 10–15 minutes, until the pastry is golden brown.

Remove from the oven and serve hot with heavy cream.

This is an American version of French *clafoutis*, but without the eggs. The batter uses more flour and has baking powder instead of eggs to lift it.

blackberry cobbler

1¾ cups all-purpose flour

¼ teaspoon apple pie spice (optional)

⅔ cup superfine sugar

a large pinch salt

4 teaspoons baking powder

1 cup milk (not fat-free)

½ teaspoon vanilla extract

½ stick unsalted butter

1½ lbs. fresh or frozen blackberries

a large, shallow, metal baking pan

Serves 4–6

Preheat the oven to 350°F.

Sift the flour, spice (if using) sugar, salt, and baking powder into a bowl. Gradually whisk in the milk and vanilla extract to make a thick batter. Let it stand for 15 minutes.

Melt the butter over gentle heat in a shallow metal baking pan. Give the rested batter a quick stir, then pour it into the pan over the melted butter. Don't worry if the butter floats around and mingles with the batter at this stage. Immediately scatter the blackberries over the batter and put the cobbler into the preheated oven to bake for about 55 minutes, or until the batter is puffed and set around the blackberries.

Remove from the oven and serve with light cream or Crème Anglaise (see page 63.)

These cheeky little puds will raise a smile as you bring them to the table. Use deep ramekins to achieve the impressive starry effect. They look spectacular and I guarantee that they taste as good as they look...

individual pear, maple, and pecan cobblers

4 small ripe pears

finely grated zest and juice of
½ a lemon

4 tablespoons maple syrup

for the maple pecan cobbler topping:

½ stick unsalted butter, chilled

1¾ cups self-rising flour

a pinch of salt

3 tablespoons maple syrup

1 scant cup milk (not fat-free)

½ cup roughly chopped pecans

a baking sheet

4 ramekins or similar individual ovenproof dishes

Serves 4

Preheat the oven to 425°F.

Peel and core the pears, then slice them thickly lengthwise (or quarter, if small and thin). Put the pears into a saucepan with the lemon zest and juice and the maple syrup. Poach gently for 10 minutes until the fruit is almost tender. Set aside.

To make the topping, rub the butter into the flour and salt until it resembles fine bread crumbs. Stir the maple syrup into the milk and add ⅔ cup only to the flour, mixing with a blunt knife to form a fairly soft, sticky dough. On a lightly floured surface, roll out until ¾-inch thick, or slightly thicker. Cut out circles using a fluted 1½–2-inch cookie cutter.

Take 4 ramekins and arrange the pear slices around the edge like a star, with the thicker ends in the center of the dish and the thinner ends pointing upwards out of the dishes. Spoon the juice evenly over the pears and anchor them with a circle of cobbler dough placed lightly in the center (the pears should poke out all around the dough). Brush the top of the cobblers with the remaining milk and sprinkle with the chopped pecans.

Place the ramekins on a baking sheet and bake in the preheated oven for 10–15 minutes, until the dough is puffed and golden brown, and the pears just browning at their tips.

Remove from the oven and serve hot with heavy cream or thick Greek yogurt.

Dark bubbling blueberries hide under a light cobbled crust of lemony polenta cake. The secret of this dish is not to spoon the blobs of topping mixture too close together—leaving a little space around each one allows the fruit to bubble up through the gaps.

blueberry and lemon polenta cobbler

1½ lbs. fresh blueberries

1 stick plus 1 tablespoon unsalted butter, at room temperature

⅓ cup superfine sugar

finely grated zest and juice of 1 lemon

½ cup sour cream

½ cup all-purpose flour

½ cup fine polenta or fine cornmeal

1 tablespoon baking powder

½ teaspoon salt

2 tablespoons honey

¼ cup superfine sugar

a large, shallow ovenproof dish

Serves 4

Preheat oven to 350°F. Butter the bottom of an ovenproof baking dish and fill it with the blueberries.

Cream the stick of butter, sugar, and lemon zest together until pale and fluffy, then beat in the sour cream. Sift the flour with the polenta, baking powder, and salt and fold into the sour cream mixture. Dot the blueberries with small spoonfuls of mixture in a very random manner, until the top of the dish has been covered. Leave about an inch of space around each one. This will give the dish its "cobbled" look, and the juices from the fruit will bubble up around the dough. Bake in the preheated oven for about 20 minutes, until the top is firm. While the cobbler is baking, prepare the butter mixture for the crust.

Put the remaining tablespoon of butter in a small saucepan with the honey, lemon juice, and sugar and melt over low heat. Pour the melted mixture over the crust.

Increase the oven to 375°F and cook for another 15–20 minutes, or until golden.

Remove from the oven and serve warm with vanilla ice cream.

A truly decadent dessert for cold winter days. The sugar melts into the cream around the bananas, making a rich and sticky sauce. Cutting the shortcake topping into little circles helps it to cook faster and looks very decorative. You could try cutting making other shapes—such as hearts, flowers, or leaves—using a variety of cookie cutters.

molasses banana cobbler

4 medium bananas

⅔ cup heavy cream or evaporated milk

2 tablespoons soft brown sugar

for the molasses shortcake topping:

1¾ cups self-rising flour

pinch of salt

½ stick unsalted butter

2 tablespoons superfine sugar

½ teaspoon ground cinnamon

3 tablespoons molasses

⅔ cup milk (not fat-free), plus extra for brushing

a medium, shallow, ovenproof dish

Serves 4

Preheat the oven to 425°F.

Peel the bananas and slice thickly. Put them in an ovenproof baking dish. Mix the cream or evaporated milk with the sugar and pour it over the bananas.

Sift the flour and salt into a bowl and rub in the butter. Mix in the sugar and cinnamon. Dissolve the molasses in the milk and quickly mix with the flour to form a soft dough. Knead this briefly on a floured surface until smooth. Pat out to a thickness of no more than ¾ inch and cut into as many 1¼-inch circles as you can, re-rolling the trimmings as necessary. Use these to cover the bananas. Brush with a little milk and bake for 15–20 minutes until well-risen and golden brown on top. Cover with a piece of foil if the shortcake is cooking too quickly and the banana is still raw.

Remove from the oven and serve warm with light cream or vanilla ice cream.

I find that freezing the raspberries first makes it easier to set them into the cobbler dough. Keep half unfrozen to pile on top of the puddings once they are cooked.

little raspberry and rose cobblers

1¼ lbs. fresh raspberries, half of them frozen

for the cobbler bases:

petals of 2 pink or red roses, washed and dried (optional)

½ stick unsalted butter, chilled

1¾ cups self-rising flour

a pinch of salt

¼ cup superfine sugar (vanilla flavored if available)

1 tablespoon rosewater extract

about ⅔ cup milk (not fat-free)

confectioners' sugar, for dusting

a nonstick muffin pan

Serves 4

Preheat the oven to 425°F.

Select the most attractive rose petals and put these to one side to use as decoration. Shred the remaining ones. Rub the butter into the flour and salt until it resembles fine bread crumbs. Stir the sugar and shredded petals into this mixture.

Stir the rosewater extract into the milk and pour into the flour, mixing with a blunt knife to a fairly soft, sticky dough. On a lightly floured surface, roll out until ½-inch thick. Cut out 4 circles (approximately 6 inches wide) that will fit the cups of a nonstick muffin pan.

Place the circles gently in the pan and carefully push the frozen raspberries into the dough. Dust with confectioners' sugar and bake in the preheated oven for 10–15 minutes, until the dough is risen and golden brown. Remove from the oven and carefully lift the cobblers out of the pan.

Serve warm with the remaining fresh raspberries, a scattering of rose petals, a dusting of confectioners' sugar, and a pitcher of heavy cream.

This deliciousy summery cobbler is covered with tiny lemon-flavored dumplings. If fresh berries are not available, frozen mixed berries will be just as good.

summer berry cobbler

2 lbs. mixed summer berries (raspberries, blueberries, small strawberries, blackberries, black currants, cherries, etc)

3 tablespoons crème de cassis (optional)

3 tablespoons sugar

for the lemon cobbler topping:

½ stick unsalted butter, chilled

1¾ cups self-rising flour

a pinch of salt

⅓ cup superfine sugar

finely grated zest of 2 lemons

about ⅔ cup milk (not fat-free)

freshly squeezed juice of 1 lemon

a medium, shallow, ovenproof dish

Serves 4–6

Preheat the oven to 400°F.

Pick over the berries, discarding any really soft or bruised fruit. Mix them with the crème de cassis (if using) and sugar and pour into an ovenproof baking dish.

Rub the butter into the flour and salt until it resembles fine bread crumbs. Stir in two thirds of the sugar and add the lemon zest. Add the milk to the flour mixture, mixing with a blunt knife to form a fairly soft, sticky dough. Knead gently on a lightly floured surface. Roll the dough into a long thin sausage and, using scissors, snip off thumbnail-size pieces. Scatter these lightly over the berries.

Mix the lemon juice with the remaining sugar and liberally brush all over the "dumplings." Bake for 15 minutes, until the pastry is golden brown and the fruit softened and bubbling.

Remove from the oven and serve hot with light cream.

bettys, crisps, slumps, and more

If you have the patience, you can crack the apricot pits and take out the kernels inside. These taste very much like bitter almonds, and are a fantastic addition when chopped and toasted with the bread crumbs.

buttered apricot betty

1½ lbs. fresh apricots or 3 x 16-oz. cans of apricots in natural juice (not syrup)

1 stick unsalted butter, cut up

3 cups fresh bread crumbs, lightly toasted

2 tablespoons corn or golden syrup

½ cup orange juice

¼ cup superfine sugar

a medium ovenproof deep pie or soufflé dish

a large roasting pan

Serves 4

Preheat the oven to 375°F.

Cut the fresh apricots in half and flip out the pits, or drain the canned apricots and pat dry. Place a layer of apricots in a buttered deep pie or soufflé dish.

Reserve 4–6 tablespoons of bread crumbs for the top. Sprinkle some of the rest of the bread crumbs over the apricots, and dot with some of the butter. Put in some more apricots and repeat these alternate casual layers until all the apricots and bread crumbs are used up. Use the reserved bread crumbs for the final top layer.

Warm the syrup with the orange juice, and pour this over the top. Sprinkle with sugar and dot with the remaining butter.

Place the pie dish in a roasting pan and pour enough boiling water in the pan to come half way up the sides of the dish. This is a "water bath." Bake in the preheated oven for 45 minutes, or until the apricots are soft and the top crispy and brown.

Remove from the oven and serve warm (not hot) with cream.

Pineapple, rum, and coconut—three flavors that are just made for each other. I often use blocks of sweetened coconut cream (available from ethnic grocery stores) for grating into desserts, as you can use the amount you like, and the rest keeps well in a plastic bag.

pineapple rum betty
with coconut and macadamia topping

1 medium fresh pineapple

1 cup shredded, unsweetened coconut

2½ oz. pound cake, crumbed

2½-oz. piece creamed coconut block, grated

¾ stick unsalted butter

4 oz. macadamia nuts, roughly chopped

2 tablespoons corn or golden syrup

½ cup dark or golden rum

a baking sheet

a medium, deep pie or soufflé dish

a large roasting pan

Serves 6

Preheat the oven to 375°F.

Cut the top and bottom off the pineapple, then cut off the skin, removing the "eyes" using the tip of a potato peeler. Cut into quarters and then take out the hard core. Slice thinly.

Spread the coconut evenly over a large baking sheet and toast in the oven for about 5 minutes, until pale golden brown. Mix with the pound cake and half of the grated creamed coconut.

Place a layer of the sliced pineapple in a deep pie or soufflé dish. Reserve 4–6 tablespoons toasted coconut mixture for the top. Sprinkle some of the rest of the coconut mixture over the pineapple, and dot with butter. Lay in some more pineapple and repeat these alternate casual layers until all the pineapple and coconut are used up. Mix the reserved coconut with the chopped macadamia nuts and use this for the final top layer.

Warm the syrup with the rum, and pour it over the top. Sprinkle with the remaining grated creamed coconut and dot with the remaining butter. Place the dish in a roasting pan and pour enough boiling water into the pan to come half way up the sides of the dish. This is a "water bath." Bake in the oven for 35–40 minutes, until the pineapple is soft and the top crispy and brown. If the top browns too much, lay a piece of foil loosely on top.

Remove from the oven and serve warm (not hot) with cream.

This is really good made in individual dishes or cups, but make sure they are ovenproof. I like to serve each guest their own little pitcher of cream so that they don't feel greedy reaching over the table for more!

cranberry and orange streusel crisp

18 oz. fresh or frozen cranberries

finely grated zest and juice of 1 orange

honey, to taste

for the streusel topping:

½ cup all-purpose flour

⅓ cup soft brown sugar

¾ stick unsalted butter, chilled

a small, shallow, ovenproof dish

Serves 4

Preheat the oven to 425°F.

Put the cranberries in a saucepan with the orange juice (not the zest) and bring to a boil. Cook for 2 minutes, then remove from the heat and sweeten to taste with honey. Pour into a baking dish and allow to cool.

Mix the flour, sugar, and orange zest in a bowl and add the butter. Rub the butter into the dry mixture until it resembles fine bread crumbs and is on no account greasy or oily. Place it in a plastic bag and leave in the fridge for 20 minutes if it has become so.

Once the cranberries are cold, sprinkle evenly with the streusel topping and bake in the preheated oven for 10 minutes, then turn down the heat to 350°F and bake for another 15 minutes.

Remove from the oven and serve warm with light cream.

My cheat's way of making caramel is to melt my favorite caramel candies in butter; this takes away all the worry of caramelizing sugar. Adding polenta or cornmeal to this crisp topping gives it a lovely crunch. It looks very homey baked in a heavy cast iron pan, but I have also cooked it in individual blini pans to great effect.

caramel apple crisp

6 medium eating apples

juice of ½ a lemon

½ stick unsalted butter

4 oz. hard caramel candies, crushed or chopped

a pinch of cinnamon

for the oat crisp topping:

½ cup polenta or cornmeal

¾ cup rolled oats (not instant)

¾ stick butter, melted

½ cup light brown sugar

a cast iron skillet (11-inches diameter) or 6 individual blini pans

Serves 6

Preheat the oven to 375°F.

Core and thickly slice the apples and toss them with the lemon juice. Melt the butter in a heavy cast iron pan or skillet that will go in the oven (or individual blini pans), then add the crushed hard caramel candies. Stir until melted, add the apples, and cinnamon, and toss well to coat in the buttery caramel mixture. Set aside.

Now make the oat topping. Put the polenta or cornmeal, oats, and sugar in a bowl and mix well. Stir in the melted butter, and work through the mixture with your fingers. The mixture will resemble rough bread crumbs. At this point you can place it in a plastic bag and chill in the fridge until needed.

Lightly sprinkle the topping mixture evenly over the surface of the apples, mounding it up a little towards the center. Bake in the preheated oven for 40 minutes or until nicely browned and crisp.

Remove from the oven and serve warm with crème fraîche, sour cream, vanilla ice cream, or Butterscotch Sauce (see page 63.)

A pandowdy is usually made with a rolled sweet dough or dough baked on top of fruit, the crust being "dowdied" by pushing the sweet dough into the fruit juices to soften it before serving. It can also be served upside down like a French *Tarte Tatin*—the key thing is that the dough will soak up some of the wonderfully fruity juices.

plum and hazelnut pandowdy

2 lbs. mixed plums

½ cup light brown sugar

½ teaspoon ground cinnamon

finely grated zest and juice of 1 small orange

3 tablespoons unsalted butter, chilled and cut up

for the pandowdy crust:

2 cups all-purpose flour

3 tablespoons superfine sugar

1 tablespoon baking powder

1 stick less 1 tablespoon unsalted butter, chilled and cut up

2½ oz. finely ground hazelnuts

about 1 cup light cream or buttermilk

superfine sugar, for dusting

a cast iron skillet or heavy baking pan (11-inches diameter)

Serves 6

Preheat the oven to 425°F.

Cut the plums in half and slice them thickly. Mix them with the sugar, cinnamon, orange zest, and juice in a bowl. Tip the fruit into a cast iron skillet or heavy baking pan. Dot with the butter.

To make the pandowdy crust, sift the flour, sugar, and baking powder into a large bowl. Rub the chilled butter into the flour until the mixture resembles coarse bread crumbs. Add the ground hazelnuts and mix. Stir in all but a couple of tablespoons of the cream or buttermilk with a blunt knife, until the dough comes together. It will be sticky. Knead very lightly until smooth. Working quickly, roll out to a circle ¼ inch thick and ½ inch wider than the pan. With the help of the rolling pin, lift the dough over the fruit and over the edge of the pan. Do not press the crust onto the sides of the pan. Make a couple of slits in the dough to allow steam to escape. Brush with the remaining cream or buttermilk and dust with sugar.

Stand the pan on a baking sheet to catch any leaking juices and bake in the preheated oven for 10 minutes, then reduce to 350°F and loosely cover with foil. Bake for a further 35–40 minutes, until the crust is golden.

Remove from the oven and "dowdy" the crust by sharply pushing it under the surface of the bubbling fruit with a large spoon. Serve warm with cream.

Here we have a real *clafoutis* originating from the Limousin area in France and made with eggs as the raising agent. When my mother baked this, the cherries were not pitted. As you ate them you would leave the pits on the side of the plate and when finished, say the rhyme "tinker, tailor, soldier, sailor, rich man, poor man, beggar man, thief" while counting them, to find out who you would marry! Ground almonds may be used instead of flour.

cherry clafoutis

2 cups milk (not fat-free)

1 vanilla bean, split, seeds scraped out and reserved

3 eggs

a pinch of salt

5 tablespoons superfine sugar

¼ cup all-purpose flour

1½ lbs. fresh or frozen cherries

½ stick unsalted butter, chilled and cut up

a little dark rum (optional)

superfine sugar, for dredging

a medium, shallow, ovenproof dish

Serves 4

Preheat the oven to 425°F.

Heat the milk and vanilla seeds to blood temperature—you should be able to hold a finger in the liquid and count to ten without any pain.

Whisk the eggs lightly with the salt and sugar until pale, then whisk in the flour. Pour in the warmed milk, stirring to mix. Scatter the cherries into a shallow ovenproof dish and pour the batter over them. Dot with pieces of butter and bake for about 25–30 minutes, or until the batter is puffed and set around the cherries.

Remove from the oven and sprinkle with rum and liberally dredge with sugar before serving warm.

I just love the word slump—it really describes the sloppy batter that covers the seasonal fruit in this satisfying dessert. Normally the fruit is on the bottom and the thick batter spooned or poured roughly over the top. I like to see more fruit, so I pour the batter in first, then push in the fruit and it works very well. You can use any juicy fruit, and berries are good too. I sometimes substitute pine nuts for almonds and sprinkle them all over the batter. You can also add a drop or two of almond extract to the batter if you like a stronger flavor.

apricot and almond slump

1 lb. 6 oz. fresh apricots

¾ light brown sugar

for the almond slump batter:

1½ cups all-purpose flour

1 tablespoon baking powder

a pinch of salt

1 cup ground almonds

about 1½ cups milk (not fat-free)

½ stick unsalted butter, melted

¼ cup whole blanched almonds

a large, non-stick, metal cake pan, buttered

Serves 4-6

Preheat the oven to 375°F.

Cut the apricots in half, remove the pits and mix with ½ cup of the sugar. Set aside until needed.

Sift together the flour, baking powder, salt, and remaining sugar into a bowl. Stir in the ground almonds, the milk, and melted butter and whisk until smooth and thick. Pour the batter into the prepared baking pan, then push in the apricots, cut side up, but in a higgledy-piggledy manner and slightly at an angle all over. Place a whole almond inside each apricot where the pit once was.

Bake the slump for 25–30 minutes in the middle of the preheated oven, until risen and golden.

Remove from the oven and allow to cool slightly before serving with vanilla ice cream.

butterscotch sauce

This makes a deliciously sticky dessert sauce. For a variation, simply stir in ⅓ cup finely chopped candied or preserved ginger.

½ stick unsalted butter

⅓ cup light brown sugar

¼ cup granulated sugar

½ cup corn or golden syrup

1¼ cups heavy cream

½ teaspoon vanilla extract

Serves 4-6

Put the butter, light brown sugar, granulated sugar, and syrup into a medium-sized pan. Stir over low heat until the sugars have dissolved and then bubble gently for 5 minutes, until smooth and thick.

Remove the pan from the heat before stirring in the heavy cream and vanilla extract. Keep warm if serving immediately.

There will be more than enough sauce for four servings but it will keep in the fridge for up to a week. Just reheat gently before serving.

crème Anglaise
(real English custard)

This classic creamy sauce is perfect with crumbles and cobblers.

1 vanilla bean

1¼ cups milk (not fat-free)

2 egg yolks

1–2 tablespoons superfine sugar

2 tablespoons brandy (cognac or Armagnac) (optional)

Serves 4

Split the vanilla bean, scrape out the seeds and reserve. Pour the milk into a saucepan, whisk in the vanilla seeds and add the vanilla bean. Bring the milk to a boil, then turn off the heat and let it infuse for 15 minutes. Remove the vanilla bean, rinse and dry it and keep for another time.

Put the egg yolks with the sugar in a bowl and whisk until pale. Pour the hot, flavored milk over them, mix well and return to the pan. Stir with a wooden spoon over very low heat until the sauce thickens enough to coat the back of the spoon. Do not allow to overheat or it will curdle.

Pour into a cold bowl to stop the cooking process and stir in the brandy, if using. Use immediately or cover the surface directly with plastic wrap (to prevent a skin from forming), cool and chill. Reheat very gently (without bringing to a boil) before serving.

index

conversion chart

Weights and measures have been rounded up
or down slightly to make measuring easier.

Measuring butter:

A US stick of butter weighs 4 oz. which is approximately
115 g or 8 tablespoons. The recipes in this book require
the following conversions:

American	Metric	Imperial
6 tbsp	85 g	3 oz.
7 tbsp	100 g	3½ oz.
1 stick	115 g	4 oz.

Volume equivalents:

American	Metric	Imperial
1 teaspoon	5 ml	
1 tablespoon	15 ml	
¼ cup	60 ml	2 fl.oz.
⅓ cup	75 ml	2½ fl.oz.
½ cup	125 ml	4 fl.oz.
⅔ cup	150 ml	5 fl.oz. (¼ pint)
¾ cup	175 ml	6 fl.oz.
1 cup	250 ml	8 fl.oz.

Weight equivalents: / Measurements:

Imperial	Metric	Inches	Cm
1 oz.	30 g	¼ inch	5 mm
2 oz.	55 g	½ inch	1 cm
3 oz.	85 g	¾ inch	1.5 cm
3½ oz.	100 g	1 inch	2.5 cm
4 oz.	115 g	2 inches	5 cm
5 oz.	140 g	3 inches	7 cm
6 oz.	175 g	4 inches	10 cm
8 oz. (½ lb.)	225 g	5 inches	12 cm
9 oz.	250 g	6 inches	15 cm
10 oz.	280 g	7 inches	18 cm
11½ oz.	325 g	8 inches	20 cm
12 oz.	350 g	9 inches	23 cm
13 oz.	375 g	10 inches	25 cm
14 oz.	400 g	11 inches	28 cm
15 oz.	425 g	12 inches	30 cm
16 oz. (1 lb.)	450 g		

Oven temperatures:

180°C	(350°F)	Gas 4
190°C	(375°F)	Gas 5
200°C	(400°F)	Gas 6
220°C	(425°F)	Gas 7